WILDE'S
LEISURE GUIDES

CYCLE ROUTE GUIDE

TO 34 LEISURE TRAILS

YORKSHIRE DALES, HUMBERSIDE AND NORTH/WEST YORKSHIRE

Written by
Gillian Rowan-Wilde

Published by

GILDERSLEVE
PUBLISHING LIMITED

ABOUT THE AUTHOR

Gillian Rowan-Wilde took up leisure cycling in the summer of 1993, her first trail being the Tarka Trail which she undertook during a holiday in Devon. Since then she has ridden most of the trails in the North West.

As well as cycling she is an accomplished fell and mountain walker. Among her accomplishments as a walker, are the completion of one of the '100' mile walks, Mountain Marathons and numerous challenge walks over 30 miles.

She has completed courses at Glencoe in Scotland on rock and ice climbing also survival techniques whilst on the mountains with instructors from the Crowden Outdoor Pursuits Centre.

In this series of guides she hopes to bring to the leisure cyclist a catalogue of historical and interesting features on rides, together with some of the wildlife you may encounter.

MAPS BY

Andy Thelwell has grown up with Apple Macs and computer graphics. At present he is employed as a technical manager with a leading north west art studio

In his spare time he is either in the gym, or out off-road on his mountain bike.

ILLUSTRATION BY

Graham Nicholson studied illustration at Lincoln, since then he has been commissioned by many leading national, and international companies, supplying work for packaging, advertising campaign's and corporate brochures.

In his leisure time he is a keen walker, an interest he shares with his family.

INTRODUCTION

Welcome to our third book which covers our selection of trails mainly in the Yorkshire Dales, Moors and Wolds.

Unlike our first guide, where the majority of trails followed disused railways, this time we guide you upward through forest and moorland. This means that some of the routes are more challenging rides through undulating country, but we hope that you'll find the spectacular views more than compensate for the climbs. For those who prefer a more leisurely ride, we've also included some trails that follow waterways, estuaries and old railway lines.

Each route has its own custom-drawn map showing everything you need to know from distances and directions to parking, picnic and rest stops.

In researching this book we have been asked by the custodians of our National Parks and Forest Enterprise to remind visitors to be mindful of the potential impact we can have on the flora and fauna on these trails, particularly in wet conditions where large numbers of users can cause erosion.

The majority of our recommended rides are on trails with reasonable surfaces with the exception of the moorland routes and we would advise that these are not undertaken in wet weather.

We have also included for the first time an accommodation listing for those who may want to stay over.

I hope you enjoy your cycling.

We're about to start book 4 which covers Devon and Cornwall and this should be published by early summer '97, until then,

Happy trails

Peter Gildersleve

GENERAL INFORMATION

Wilde's Leisure Guides are a trade mark of Gildersleve Publishing Ltd.

© Copyright Gillian Rowan-Wilde

Published by
Gildersleve Publishing Ltd
Capricorn House, Blackburn Road
Rising Bridge, Lancashire BB5 2AA

ACKNOWLEDGMENTS
To Mr Karl Gerhardsen, Public Rights of Way Officer for the North York Moors National Park. Mr B. Walker, Head Recreation Ranger, North York Moors Forest District, Forestry Commission. M. Clements, Director of Technical Services, Scarborough Borough Council. Mrs Bev Parker, Access Officer for the Yorkshire Dales National Park, and Mr Andrew Hardwick, Chief Engineer, Rochdale Canal Company, for their advice and help in checking the routes in their specific areas.

Last but not least the originators of all the trails without which it would have been impossible to start this journey.

Maps based upon Ordinance Survey mapping with the permission of the Controller of Her Majesty's Stationery, Office, © Crown copyright.

THE OFFROAD CYCLING CODE

STAY ON THE TRAIL
Only ride bridleways & byways
Avoid footpaths
Plan your route in advance

GIVE WAY TO HORSES & WALKERS
Make sure you are heard when riding up behind anyone
Ride Carefully, keep to the left of anyone approaching you.

NEVER RIDE IN LARGE GROUPS
5 or 6 is maximum

BE KIND TO BIRDS, ANIMALS & PLANTS
Keep your dog under control

PREVENT EROSION
Avoid skidding and locking your wheels when braking.

CLOSE GATES BEHIND YOU
Don't climb walls or force hedges

EQUIPMENT FOR SAFETY
Wear a helmet
Take a first aid kit
Carry enough food and drink
Pack waterproofs & warm clothes
Take essential spares & tools

TAKE PRIDE IN YOUR BIKE
Maintain your bike before you leave, and on your return.

BE TIDY
Take all your litter home
Never create a fire hazard

ENJOY YOUR CYCLING
Try not to get annoyed with anyone, it never solves a problem Don't make unnecessary noise

RIGHTS OF WAY

Off-road cyclists have right of way on most public bridleways and other tracks unless forbidden by a bye-law. You must give way to walkers and horseriders.

By-ways, which are usually unsurfaced tracks are open to cyclists, as well as walkers and horseriders, you may also find vehicles have right to access.

There is NO right of way on Public Footpaths, if cyclists finds themselves on a public footpath they must get off their bike and walk.

A cyclist is NOT permitted to ride his bike on the pavements.

On moorland, upland or farmland a cyclist normally has NO right of access without the express permission of the landowner.

Tow-paths by the canals normally require a permit from the appropriate British Waterways.

There are quite a few designated cycle routes and paths to be found in urban areas, on Waterways tow-paths, Forestry Commission land or on disused railway lines.

Cyclists must adhere to the Highway Code.

GENERAL SAFETY HINTS

1. Make sure your bike is safe to ride before leaving home. It is adviseable to take with you a puncture repair kit, a spare inner tube, and the necessary spanners and levers to help with your repair. Don't forget your pump!

2. You must by law display working lights after dark.

3. Always carry some form of identification.

4. Always tell someone where you are going.

5. Learn the basic principles of first aid and take a small first aid kit.

6. Wear reflective material on your clothes, better to be seen.

7. Ride under control when going down hill, accidents can happen.

8. It is adviseable to always wear a helmet.

9. Carry a water bottle, always keep it filled especially on a hot day. Take spare food, drink and clothing with you.

10. Be very careful when riding on marsh land or scree especially when it is wet.

11. Always take a detailed map with you for adventurous or wilderness trips. Have a compass with you. Take a whistle with you to use when calling for help should you have an accident.

12. Always be aware of others using the same path as yourself. They also want to enjoy their day out!

13. General maintenance of your bike on your return home. Making sure it is cleaned and oiled ready for your next trip.

3

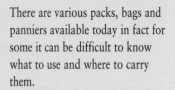

PACKING YOUR ESSENTIALS

There are various packs, bags and panniers available today in fact for some it can be difficult to know what to use and where to carry them.

Illustrated are a number of carrying positions for different capacities of bags. In addition to these there are a variety of touring front and rear panniers available. Coming from a walking background I prefer to use a small daysac in which I carry my food and waterproofs with a bar bag on the bike which usually has my tool kit, chocolate, maps and camera. Other people I know prefer to keep their body free and carry everything on their bikes - so you should do which ever feels comfortable.

Bar Bag • Bum Bag • Rucksack

Bar Bag • Rack Pack

Stem Bag • Wedge Bag • Seat Bag

CONTENTS

KEY

i Information Centre

P Parking

PC Public Convenience

☎ Telephone

⚎ Picnic Area

△ Camp Site

⊞ Caravan Site

⚏ Public House/Hotel

⚓ Boating

✝ Church

⚑ Mill

Built up Area

Quarry

Cycle Trail
Main Road
Minor Road
Footpath
Railway Track
National Park Boundary

River/Stream

Lake/Reservoir

Mixed Wood

Coniferous Wood

Erosion

TRAIL LOCATION MAP

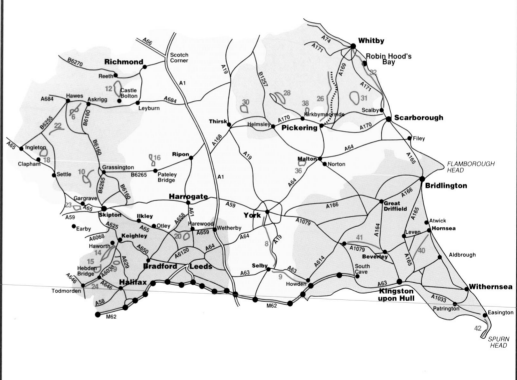

—— Trail *(page No)*
North Yorkshire
Yorkshire Dales

North York Moors
West Yorkshire
Humberside

CAM HIGH ROAD

(Roman Road)

THIS ROMAN ROAD IS SITUATED EAST OF SLEDDALE AND WEST OF RAYDALE. THE A684 IS TO THE NORTH WITH LANGSTROTHDALE CHASE TO THE SOUTH.

The Cam High road was the link between the Roman Legion's fort of Virosidvm on Brough Hill just outside Bainbridge, and the major fort at Lancaster. This amazing straight walled road can be seen for miles as it makes its way over the moors. This section of Cam High Road is 5 miles long and finishes on Beggermans Road.

(S1) The route begins on the Roman Road where it meets the Countersett road out of Bainbridge *(turning right on a sharp bend)*. Follow this straight route for 3 miles, turning left at the first Bridleway sign, through the gate and onto the open moors. Follow the very distinctive grass track across the open fell which finally descends to the minor road north of Countersett, turn left up the hill and return by way of the Roman Road. The lake of Semer Water, down in the valley of Rydale, has a sunken village complete with church bells that have been heard to toll on stormy days.

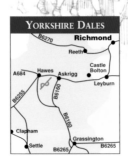

YORKSHIRE DALES

Cam High Road looking towards Wether Hill.

START & FINISH: (1)		The Roman Road (Bainbridge to Countersett)
S (2)		Beggermans Road (Hawes to Oughtershaw)
MAP :		O.S.Outdoor Leisure 30 Yorkshire Dales (North/Central)
LENGTH (approx) :		1) 11km (7 m) Circular (Semer Water)
		2) 8 km (5 m) Circular (Wether Fell)
SURFACE :		1&2 - Grass/gravel
RIDE RATING :		Moderate adverturous

(S2) The trail contours Wether Hill. The views of the surrounding hills and moors are magnificent and include many of the 'dales' such as Wensleydale, Rydale, Sleddale and Widdale. To the north is the village of Hawes on the River Ure where the famous Wensleydale cheese is produced.

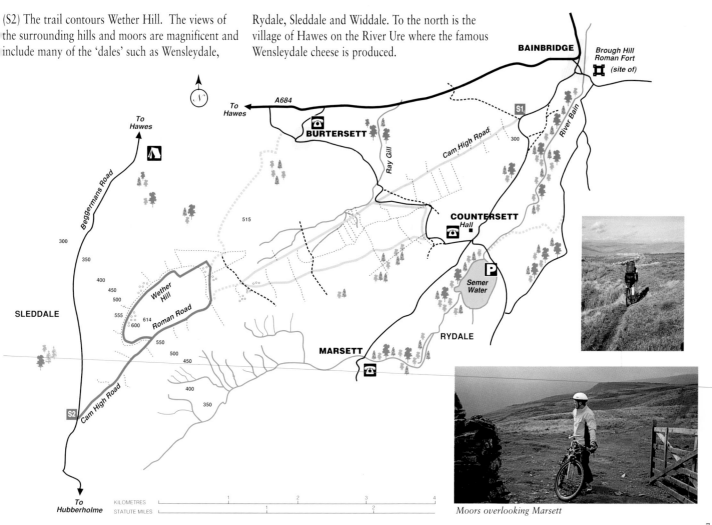

BAINBRIDGE

Brough Hill
Roman Fort
(site of)

To
Hawes

A684

BURTERSETT

S1

Cam High Road

300

River Bain

Ray Gill

COUNTERSETT
Hall

To
Hawes

Beggermans Road

P

Semer
Water

515

300

350

400

450

500

Wether
Hill

555   614

600

Roman Road

550

RYDALE

SLEDDALE

500

MARSETT

450

S2   Cam High Road

400

350

To
Hubberholme

KILOMETRES   1   2   3   4
STATUTE MILES   1   2

Moors overlooking Marsett

7

YORK - SELBY
RAILWAY PATH

THIS ROUTE IS LOCATED BETWEEN THE CITY OF YORK AND THE TOWN OF SELBY. THE A19(T) LIES TO THE EAST PROVIDING SEVERAL ACCESS POINTS TO THE TRAIL, WITH THE RIVER OUSE TO THE WEST OF THE PATH.

The trail commences beside the River Ouse in the heart of the City of York, on past the Racecourse and down through Bishopthorpe. The track continues over the Swing Bridge at Naburn and on through wonderful open countryside with views of the River Ouse as it flows down to Selby. The trail through to Selby follows the route of the old railway line which was closed in 1983 and opened as a traffic-free route in June 1989.

This path is part of Sustrans Trans-Pennine Trail, a 240km leisure route from Liverpool to Hull.

Trans Pennine Trail

START :	**S**	Terry Avenue, York (Beside the River Ouse)
FINISH :		The Toll Bridge, Selby
MAP :		O.S. Landranger 105 York
LENGTH (approx) :		24 km (15m) Linear
SURFACE :		Tarmac/gravel
RIDE RATING :		Easy

NOTES : *To continue the trail to Howden follow the 'Trans Pennine Trail' signs over the Toll Bridge at Selby*

KILOMETRES
STATUTE MILES

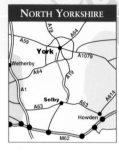

NORTH YORKSHIRE

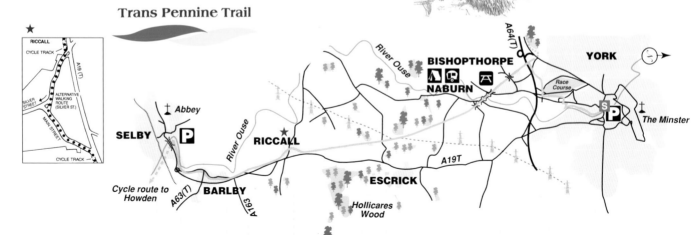

SELBY - HOWDEN

THIS ROUTE IS SITUATION BETWEEN SELBY AND HOWDEN. THE A63(T) RUNS TO THE NORTH AND THE RIVER OUSE TO THE SOUTH. THIS TRAIL IS PART OF SUSTRAN'S TRANS-PENNINE TRAIL WHICH WILL EVENTUALLY BECOME A CONTINUOUS LEISURE TRAIL FROM LIVERPOOL TO KINGSTON UPON HULL

The trail begins on the right immediately after the Toll Bridge, on the north side of the River Ouse. The path follows the river to Turnham Hall, then a short detour (very well marked with the Trans-Pennine Trail signs) on to a specially made track for cyclists and pedestrians beside the A63(T). Through the attractive village of Hemingbrough with its beautiful tall steepled church and outside the church you will notice the worn stone mounting block.

The track returns to follow the river bank and marshes with its variety of wildlife and extensive views over the river and neighbouring farmlands.

START :	[S] Toll Bridge, Selby
FINISH :	Kilpin Pike, Howden
MAP :	O.S. Landranger 105 York
LENGTH (approx) :	16 km (10 m) Linear
SURFACE :	Tarmac/gravel
RIDE RATING :	Easy

NOTES : At Barmby Tidal Barrage - cyclists must dismount and wheel bikes across.

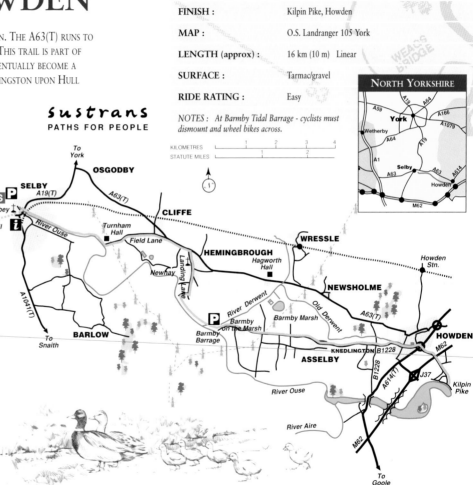

HETTON COMMON

HETTON COMMON IS SITUATED NORTH OF THE VILLAGES OF HETTON AND WINTERBURN. WITH 'THE WEETS' AT A HEIGHT OF 414M TO THE WEST. BOSS MOOR AND THE VILLAGE OF THRESHFIELD ON THE B6265 TO THE EAST.

(S1) The trail has a gradual climb of 150m from Skirethorns Lane on a track up onto the moor to Boss Moor Lane. The views are worth all the effort - they are superb! The trails are grassy bridleway tracks easily signposted over beautiful moorlands.

(S2) The trail starts on Boss Moor Lane an ancient drovers road used by travellers between towns and traders taking their livestock to market. The view across the valley to Winterburn Moor is wonderous and the bridleway wending its way beside Whetstone Gill over the hill to Malham makes one think how difficult and dangerous travelling from town-to-town on these fells must have been in days gone by. Follow the trail to a four track crossing. Through the gate on your right and down through the trees to Long Hill Farm. Follow the waymarked posts across the fields down to a hollow (very muddy) and through the gate in the corner of the field. Keep the farm buildings on your right and go through the gate into a walled grassy lane. Follow this track round into Cross Lane and either follow Moor Lane up the hill back to the four track crossing or return via Fleets Lane.

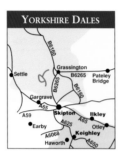

YORKSHIRE DALES

START :	**S** (1) Skirethorns Lane, Threshfield
	(2) Boss Moor Lane (Off Fleets Lane)
FINISH :	(1) & (2) Boss Moor Lane
MAP :	O.S. Outdoor Leisure 10 Yorkshire Dales (South)
LENGTH (approx) :	(1) 5½ km (3 ½ m) Linear
	(2) 9 km (5 ½ m) Circular
SURFACE :	Tarmac/grass/gravel
RIDE RATING :	(1) & (2) Moderate

NOTES : Be aware of the weather on these moorlands as the mist comes down very quickly on the open fells.

KILOMETRES

STATUTE MILES

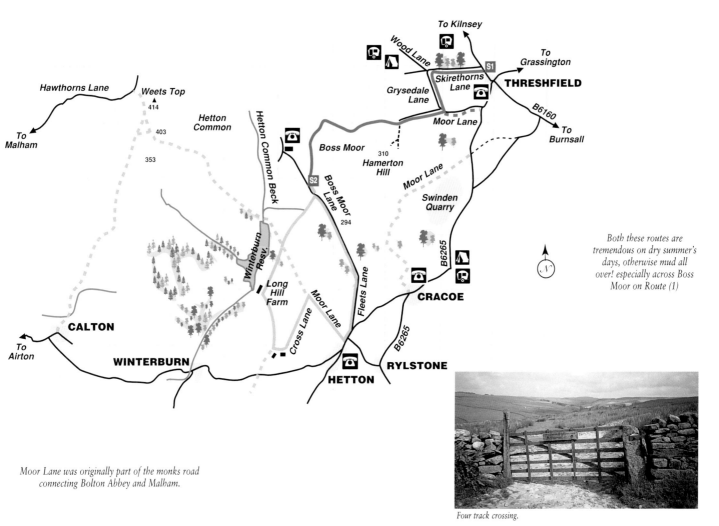

Hawthorns Lane

To Malham

Weets Top
▲ 414
403
353

Hetton Common

Hetton Common Beck

S2

Boss Moor Lane

294

Winterburn Resv.

Long Hill Farm

Moor Lane

Cross Lane

CALTON

To Airton

WINTERBURN

HETTON

RYLSTONE

Fleets Lane

To Kilnsey

Wood Lane

Skirethorns Lane

Grysedale Lane

Moor Lane

THRESHFIELD

S1

B6160

To Grassington

To Burnsall

Boss Moor

310
Hamerton Hill

Moor Lane

Swinden Quarry

B6265

CRACOE

B6265

N

Both these routes are tremendous on dry summer's days, otherwise mud all over! especially across Boss Moor on Route (1)

Moor Lane was originally part of the monks road connecting Bolton Abbey and Malham.

Four track crossing.

BOLTON CASTLE

The village of Castle Bolton is situated north of the River Ure in Wensleydale on a minor road between Leyburn and Carperby in the district of Richmondshire.

Some of the most scenic moorland can be found between the River Ure that tumbles down through the valley of Wensleydale and the River Swale in Swaledale.

The grandeur of Bolton Castle dominates this part of the valley of Wensleydale, it took eighteen years to build and was completed in 1568. In July of that year until January 1569, Mary Queen of Scots was held prisoner at the Castle, following her defeat at Langside, until her eventual journey south to Fotheringhay where she was later beheaded.

This trail starts by turning left between the houses at the bridleway sign. The hill up behind these houses is quite hard but once on the hill top the picturesque valley of Apedale can be seen before you.

Descend to Dents Houses, over the bridge that spanes Apedale Beck and turn left at junction with the metalled road. Follow this very attractive dale along the beck to the head of the valley. At the junction of bridleways keep to the right hand track as it follows round to Harkerside Moor.

YORKSHIRE DALES

START & FINISH:	**S**	Bolton Castle car park
MAP :		Outdoor Leisure 30 Yorkshire Dales (North/Central)
LENGTH (approx) :		18 km (12 m) Circular
SURFACE :		Grass/tarmac/gravel
RIDE RATING :		Hard

KILOMETRES
STATUTE MILES

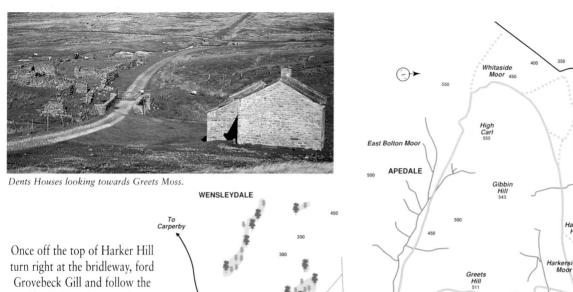

Dents Houses looking towards Greets Moss.

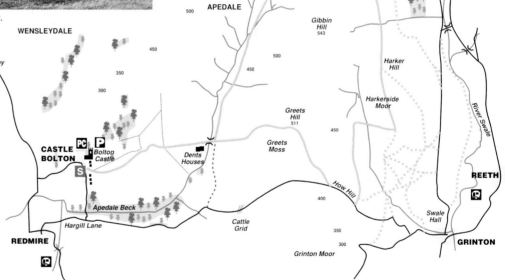

Once off the top of Harker Hill turn right at the bridleway, ford Grovebeck Gill and follow the track uphill to the top, where the track turns left onto a grassy track to the road at How Hill. Turn right and follow the road up hill to a clearing on your right where there is a bridleway sign taking you to Greets Hill and down to Dents Houses. Keep straight ahead at the junction in Apedale, over the meadow and back down to the village of Castle Bolton.

In the valley of Swaledale, between the heather and juniper growing on Harkerside Moor are the remains of numerous lead mining activities of two centuries ago.

HAWORTH -
BRONTË COUNTRY
STAIRS LANE

This trail takes the southerly route out of Haworth. The A6033 road from Haworth to Oxenhope lies to the east and the Moors of Haworth and Wadsworth to the west.

The story of the Brontë sisters sets the tone of this ride by beginning the trail at The Parsonage, where the Brontë family lived, and continue by either turning right and going down the hill of the narrow cobbled High Street of Haworth to Marsh Lane, or by turning left at the High Street and going round by Penistone Hill, giving two alternative ways of seeing this historic area. From Lee Lane the climb to the 'Top of Stairs' is well worth the effort as the views all around of the moors are excellent. If you are feeling very energetic, once on the 'Old Road', continue to the Hebden Dale Horseshoe! *(page 15)*

START :	**S** Brontë Parsonage Car Park, Haworth, West Yorkshire
FINISH :	Haworth Old Road - Top of Stairs Lane
MAP :	O.S. Outdoor Leisure 21 South Pennines
LENGTH (approx) :	8 km (5m) Linear
SURFACE :	Tarmac/stoney moorland
RIDE RATING :	Moderate

NOTES : *This moorland route can get very wet along the 'Top of Stairs' after a wet season.*

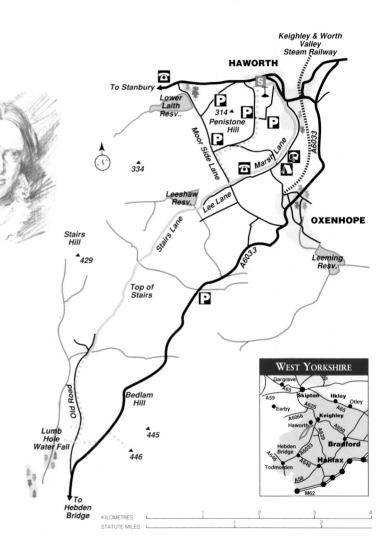

HEBDEN DALE HORSESHOE

Hebden Bridge off the A6033 is situated south of this route. To the north is Shackleton Moor. Heptonstall Moor lies to the west and the A6033 from Hebden Bridge to Oxenhope to the east.

In all seasons, the woods around Hebden Water are very picturesque and together with the open vistas on the moors around Shackleton Knoll the area is shown off to its best advantage. Once down at the waterfall at Lumb Hole, either take the Old Road to Haworth (Haworth - Stairs Lane trail), or return to the car park at New Bridge. As a picnic suggestion - follow the footpath trail beside the river to Hardcastle Crags via a restored early cotton mill on Hebden Water. It is an excellent walk and is well worth the effort.

START & FINISH	Hebden Dale N.T. Car Park, New Bridge or at Clough Foot Car Park
MAP :	O.S. Outdoor Leisure 21 South Pennines
LENGTH (approx) :	13 km (8 1/2 m) Circular
SURFACE :	Forest tracks/tarmac
RIDE RATING :	Moderate

NOTES : Care must be taken over the exposed areas of the moors as it can be very boggy after a wet season.

UPPER NIDDERDALE VALLEY

THE UPPER NIDDERDALE VALLEY TO PATELEY BRIDGE IS NORTH OF THE GRASSINGTON TO RIPON ROAD (B6265). THE YORKSHIRE DALES NATIONAL PARK TO THE WEST AND FOUNTAINS ABBEY TO THE EAST.

The source of the River Nidd is on the slopes of Great Whernside in the Yorkshire Dales National Park and flows into the River Ouse over 50 miles away. The fells above Nidderdale boasts some of the most beautiful scenery, whilst the valley is one of the most interesting in Yorkshire.
Wath village possesses one of the smallest places of worship in England, a Chapel built in 1859 measuring only 25ft by 21ft.

Route (1) On the Wath-Pateley Bridge road pass the Sportsmens Arms on your left, then as the road bends to the right, turn left up a gravel path into the woods, over the hill and down onto a track that was once the Nidd Valley Light Railway built by the Bradford Corporation in 1904 to carry materials needed to build the Angram and Scar House Reservoirs so that water could be provided for the City of Bradford.

Gouthwaite reservoir is a very picturesque stretch of water and a haven for over 200 different birds. At the pretty village of Ramsgill, turn left over the bridge to the village green on your left, turn right and follow the Nidderdale way to Lofthouse, where the spectacular 70ft high rocky cliffs of the How Stean Gorge are situated.

Route (2) From Wath turn right towards Ramsgill and following the signs for the Nidderdale way, turning sharp left through a gate (if you go over a bridge and and a track to Gouthwaite Farm you have gone too far!), up the lane passing Pie Gill farm on the left. Continue to a road junction and turn right signposted 'Bridleway to Mosscarr'. Follow the banks of Ashfold Side Beck to the old lead mine workings at Merryfield. The trail follows the clearly defined waymarked route over the Beck and past the fir tree woods on to the very pleasant track that meets the Greenhow Hill road down to Pateley Bridge. Turn left at the garage before the bridge over the Nidd back to Wath.

Gouthwaite Reservoir.

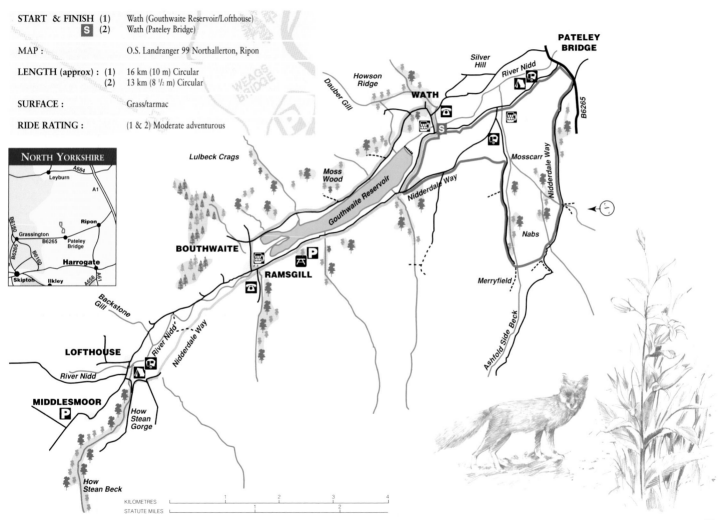

START & FINISH (1)   Wath (Gouthwaite Reservoir/Lofthouse)
     S (2)   Wath (Pateley Bridge)

MAP :   O.S. Landranger 99 Northallerton, Ripon

LENGTH (approx) : (1)   16 km (10 m) Circular
      (2)   13 km (8 ½ m) Circular

SURFACE :   Grass/tarmac

RIDE RATING :   (1 & 2) Moderate adventurous

NORTH YORKSHIRE

Leyburn
A684
A1
Ripon
Grassington
B6285 B6160
Pateley Bridge
B6265
Harrogate
Skipton
Ilkley
A59
A658 A61

PATELEY BRIDGE
Silver Hill
River Nidd
Howson Ridge
Dauber Gill
WATH
S
Mosscarr
Nidderdale Way
Lulbeck Crags
Moss Wood
Gouthwaite Reservoir
Nidderdale Way
Nabs
BOUTHWAITE
RAMSGILL
Merryfield
Backstone Gill
River Nidd
Nidderdale Way
Ashfold Side Beck
LOFTHOUSE
River Nidd
MIDDLESMOOR
How Stean Gorge
How Stean Beck

KILOMETRES   1   2   3   4
STATUTE MILES   1   2

17

NORBER HILL CIRCULAR

This route is situated north of the A65(T) the Settle to Kirkby Londsdale road. Ingleborough and Simon Fell to the north west and Ribblesdale to the east.

The terrain of this route is varied but very exciting. Having travelled through the tunnel at the beginning of this trail and up the stony track on to Thwaite Lane, the view looking north west of Ingleborough standing at 724m, is breathtaking.

At Mill Bridge turn left taking the track along the bank of Austwick Beck, through the farm to the village of Wharfe. Turn left between the houses at the bridleway signpost and up the hill to Crummack Lane.

Once past the farm at Crummack and off the metalled road follow the wall to the bridleway signpost directing you left up the hill over Crummack Dale. Follow this grassy track keeping to the right hand path as it goes up the hill towards the rocky outcrop of limestone. Down to the junction of bridleways, turn left and enjoy the exhilarating descent on the grassy fell past Long Scar.

Crummack Dale with Pen-y-ghent in the distance.

START & FINISH : **S**	Clapham - Information car park
MAP :	O.S. Outdoor Leisure 2 Yorkshire Dales (West)
LENGTH (approx) :	12 km (8 m) Circular
SURFACE :	Gravel/grass
RIDE RATING :	Hard

A little care down the stony track of Long Lane is advisable.

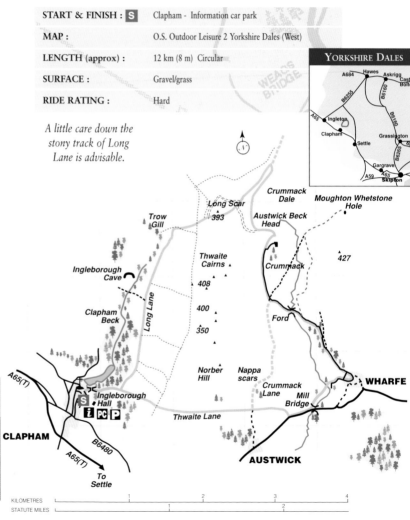

OGDEN RESERVOIR

Ovenden Moor and Ogden Reservoir are situated west of the A629, Halifax to Denholme road in West Yorkshire.

There is a wide variety of terrain on this route with magnificent views from Hambleton Lane, Hollin Hill and the surrounding moors and reservoirs. The moors are wonderfully grassy until Sawood Lane/White Moor Lane, which is stoney (*beware often wet and icy in winter*). Riding up the cobbled road past the wind machines on Old Fly Delph is certainly an experience. At the Withens Pub the BW route (also marked as a FP) is at the back of the car park and continues down a wide track to the dam wall on the Ogden reservoir.

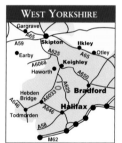

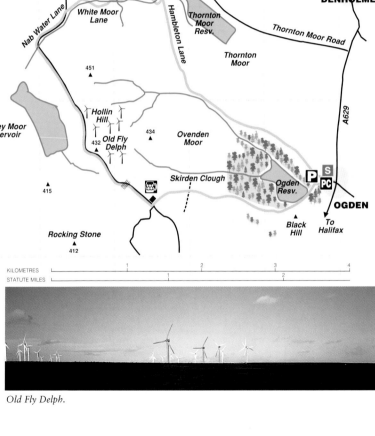

Old Fly Delph.

START & FINISH S	Ogden Reservoir Car Park
MAP :	O.S. Outdoor Leisure 21 South Pennines
LENGTH (approx) :	11 km (7 m) Circular
SURFACE :	Tarmac/cobbles/gravel/grass
RIDE RATING :	Moderate adventurous

NOTES : *This route is over open moorland and mists can roll in very quickly. Care must be taken on Hambleton Lane as it is a very popular route for walkers.*

HAREWOOD HOUSE

HAREWOOD HOUSE IS SITUATED BETWEEN HARROGATE AND LEEDS ON THE A61 AND SOUTH OF THE A659 OTLEY TO WETHERBY ROAD.

THIS TRAIL IS MAINLY ON WIDE SANDY TRACKS THROUGH BEAUTIFUL WOODED AREAS AND OPEN PARK LAND WITHIN THE HAREWOOD ESTATE. THE BRIDLEWAY SECTION OFF THE A659, ALTHOUGH MORE TAXING, IS A WONDERFUL RIDE THROUGH OPEN COUNTRYSIDE.

Tracks within Harewood House Estate.

The marvellous wrought iron gates at the beginning of this route set the scene for this trail, and the surrounding parkland allows excellent views of the very grandiose front and terraces of the 18th century mansion of Harewood House. When Edwin Lascelles built the House in 1759, he had the village of Harewood re-build outside the grounds, except for the church that was left within the estate boundary.

The bridleway through the Park is very well marked and shows off some of the spectacular scenery. Once past the Harewood House, and across the cattle grid keep right and follow the road into the village of Harewood.

Approximately 1 mile out of Harewood village on the A659 there is a lay-by on your left and a turning on your right signposted as a bridleway and New Laithe Farm. Take the left hand fork through the farmyard and keep on the track down the field. Keep to the right of Hollin Hall, across the dam of the small lake and having gone through the gate beside the wood follow the track up the hill keeping the wood to the left. Care must be taken here as the way marked arrows are not easy to find. Go up the hill and stay on the track as it veers right across to the gate in the corner of the field. Keep close to the fence on your left and on meeting a track (Leeds Country Way) turn right, then follow the track as it turns left to meet the Wike road, turn right back to the start point.

START & FINISH : **S**	A61 (to Leeds) 1 mile south of Harewood Village
MAP :	O.S. Landranger 104 Leeds & Bradford
LENGTH (approx) :	16 km (10 m) Circular
SURFACE :	Sandy track/tarmac/grass
RIDE RATING :	Moderate

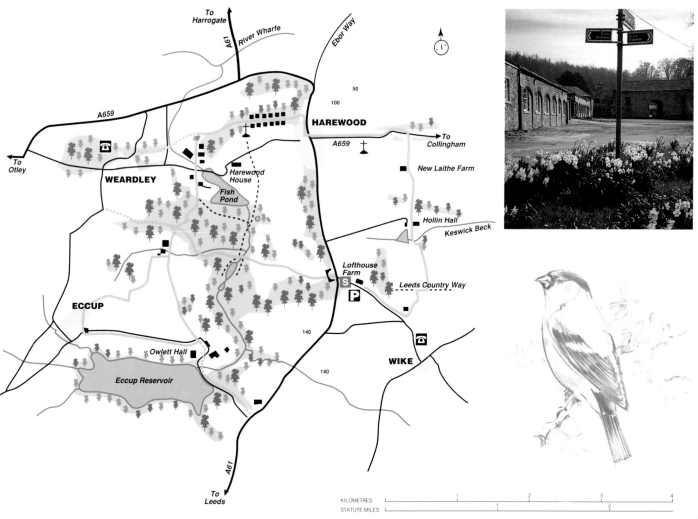

To Harrogate

A61

River Wharfe

Ebor Way

50

100

HAREWOOD

A659

To Collingham

A659

New Laithe Farm

To Otley

WEARDLEY

Harewood House

Fish Pond

Hollin Hall

Keswick Beck

ECCUP

Lofthouse Farm

S

P

Leeds Country Way

140

WIKE

Owlett Hall

Eccup Reservoir

140

A61

To Leeds

KILOMETRES   1   2   3   4

STATUTE MILES   1   2

21

GREENFIELD FOREST
(LANGSTROTHDALE)

THE TRAIL STARTS AT THE CONFLUENCE OF THE RIVER WHARFE AND GREENFIELD BECK AT BECKERMONDS, OFF THE ROAD BETWEEN BUCKDEN AND OUGHTERSHAW IN LANGSTROTHDALE CHASE. TO THE WEST LIES THE PENNINE WAY AND HORTON-IN-RIBBLESDALE, WITH OUGHTERSHAW MOSS TO THE NORTH. PLOVER HILL AND PEN-Y-GHENT ARE SOUTH OF THE TRAIL.

This route is a very attractive one through the Greenfields Foresty estate, with magnificent views of Simon Fell and Ingleborough. A considerable amount of pot holing is done in the surrounding area and along the trail there are several outcrops of limestone, showing how over the years, the weather has shaped the rock.

(An ideal young family ride especialy with a picnic)

START :	**S**	Beckermonds
FINISH :		Merging of the Trail and the Pennine Way
MAP :		O.S. Outdoor Leisure 2 Yorkshire Dales (West)
LENGTH (approx) :		8 km (5 m) Linear
SURFACE :		Tarmac/gravel
RIDE RATING :		Easy/Undulating

KILOMETRES
STATUTE MILES

YORKSHIRE DALES

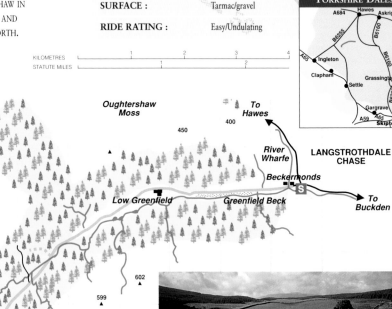

Oughtershaw Moss

To Hawes

450

400

River Wharfe

LANGSTROTHDALE CHASE

Beckermonds

S

To Buckden

Low Greenfield

Greenfield Beck

602

599

348

386

510

Pennine Way

To Horton in Ribblesdale

The trail below Low Greenfield with Ingleborough in the distance.

EAST MARTON CANTER

THIS TRAIL IS SITUATED NORTH OF THE A59(T) CLITHEROE TO SKIPTON ROAD AND SOUTH OF THE A65(T) HELLIFIELD TO GARGRAVE ROAD. THE LEEDS & LIVERPOOL CANAL AND PENNINE WAY LIE TO THE EAST, WITH THE RIVER RIBBLE TO THE WEST.

The start of this route is on a track descending through the trees and down the minor road past Stainton Hall. Keep left at the road junction then turn right through the gate onto the bridleway. These pastures are frequently used by horse riders cantering over the grass or just enjoying the beautiful scenery at a more leisurely pace. Along the bridleway from Pot Haw Farm to Bank Newton there are excellent views of the surrounding hills. At East Marton there is a double arched bridge over the canal, an excellent piece of early engineering, which now carries the A59 from Clitheroe to Skipton.

START & FINISH : [S]	East Marton (off the A59)
MAP :	O.S. Landranger 103 Blackburn/Burnley
LENGTH (approx) :	12 km (8 m) Circular
SURFACE :	Gravel/tarmac/grass
RIDE RATING :	Moderate, adverturous

NOTE : *The bridleways on this route are frequently used. Overtake the horses with care.*

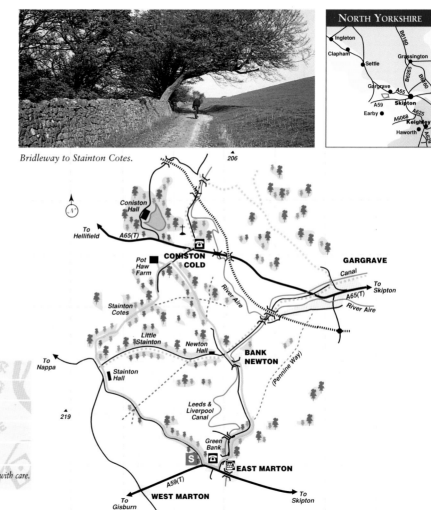

Bridleway to Stainton Cotes.

KILOMETRES 1 2 3 4
STATUTE MILES 1 2

ROCHDALE CANAL

(TODMORDEN - HEBDEN BRIDGE)

THE ROCHDALE CANAL IS 32 MILES LONG GOING IN A NORTH EASTERLY DIRECTION OUT OF THE CITY OF MANCHESTER OVER THE PENNINES TO SOWERBY BRIDGE, NEAR HALIFAX IN WEST YORKSHIRE.

The canal opened in December 1804 and was a major feat of engineering with its 92 locks, rising at the summit to 600 ft above sea level. Although the whole length of the canal is cyclable, the canal is not navigable from Todmorden to Manchester, at the moment, but since the opening of the tunnel and lock at Sowerby Bridge on 2nd May 1996 the Rochdale Canal now joins the Calder & Hebble Navigation and the national canal network. The canal is very picturesque, with many species of ducks to see along the route. Along the towpath there are places to buy refreshment, whilst you watch the canal and its wild life pass by.

The dotted brown trail is an alternative route back to Todmorden. Although a very good road and track, due to the height obtained it is considerably harder than the canal trail.

START :	S	Car Park, Union Street South, Todmorden
FINISH :		Hebden Bridge Marina
MAP :		O.S. Outdoor Leisure 21 South Pennines
LENGTH (approx) :		8 km (5 ½ m) Linear
SURFACE :		Gravel
RIDE RATING :		Easy/Dotted brown trail - Hard

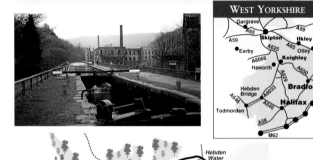

WEST YORKSHIRE

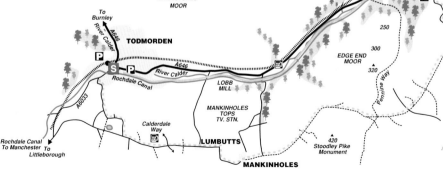

A bicycle permit is required to cycle along the towpath. Contact the Rochdale Canal Co., 75 Dale Street, Manchester, M1 2HG or Tel: 0161 236 2456

GROSMONT STEAM TRAIL
"HEARTBEAT COUNTRY" (CROPTON FOREST)

THIS TRAIL IS SITUATED NORTH OF THE A170 HELMSLEY TO SCARBOROUGH ROAD AND SOUTH OF WHEELDALE MOOR WITH THE A169 TO THE EAST AND SPAUNTON MOOR TO THE WEST.

Part of the excitement of this route is the journey on the North Yorkshire Moors Railway, which was originally constructed by George Stephenson in the 1830's. The excitement of passing through the forested valley of Newton Dale, being dwarfed by the 400ft high cliffs of the gorge, watching the engine as she steams round the edge of Cropton Forest and out onto the open fells to Goathland Station, which has barely changed since it was opened in July 1865 and on to Grosmont (*pronounced Growmont*) was only surpassed by the exhilarating return cycle trail to Pickering.

Route (1) begins at Grosmont Station on the road to Egton, under two railway bridges, turn left to ford the river and up onto Lease Rigg, over Murk Mine Moor and into Cropton forest at Mauley Cross junction. The trail meanders through Cropton forest down Newton Banks and onto the bridleway as it enters the woods south of Newton-on-Rawcliffe, eventually joining Yates road and back into Pickering.

Route (2) follow the quiet roads from Grosmont to Goathland and return on the train to Pickering.

Route (3) is a beautiful forest trail from Newtondale Halt to Levisham Station.

START & FINISH	**S**	Pickering Steam Railway Station
MAP :		O.S. North York Moors 27 (East)
LENGTH (approx) :		(1) Brown 32 km (18 m) Linear (Grosmont - Pickering)
		(2) Purple 13 km (8 m) Linear (Grosmont - Goathland)
		(3) Red 6 km (4 m) Linear (Newtondale Halt - Levisham Stn.)
SURFACE :		Forest tracks/tarmac
RIDE RATING :		(1) Moderate adventurous (2) Moderate (3) Easy

NOTES : *Check when buying your ticket that there is a space in the guard's van for your bike!* (Tel: 01751 472508)

The "Dame Vera Lynn" steaming towards Goathland.

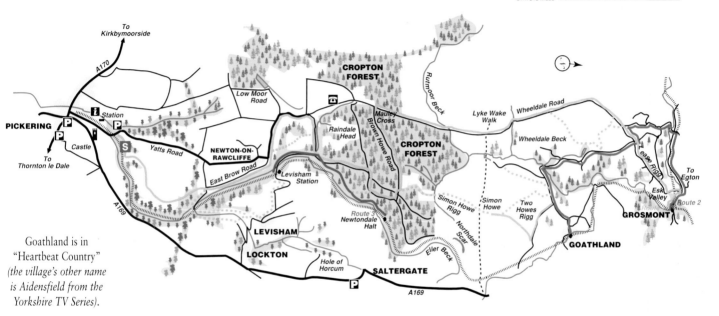

KILOMETRES 1 2 3 4
STATUTE MILES 1 2

To Kirkbymoorside

A170

CROPTON FOREST

Low Moor Road

Rumoor Beck

Lyke Wake Walk

Wheeldale Road

PICKERING

Station

Castle

To Thornton le Dale

Yatts Road

NEWTON-ON-RAWCLIFFE

East Brow Road

Levisham Station

Mauley Cross

Raindale Head

Brown Howe Road

CROPTON FOREST

Wheeldale Beck

To Egton

Esk Valley

Route 2

GROSMONT

A169

LEVISHAM

LOCKTON

Route to Newtondale Halt

Simon Howe Rigg

Simon Howe

Two Howes Rigg

GOATHLAND

Hole of Horcum

SALTERGATE

Northdale Scar

Eller Beck

A169

Lease Rigg

Goathland is in "Heartbeat Country" *(the village's other name is Aidensfield from the Yorkshire TV Series).*

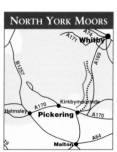

NORTH YORK MOORS

Whitby

Kirkbymoorside

Helmsley

Pickering

Malton

Signpost in the village of Goathland ("Aidensfield")

Forest Enterprise

Forest Enterprise part of the Forestry Commission

Forest Enterprise woods are managed with multi-purpose objectives, including conservation, recreation and the production of a sustainable supply of timber. Please obey any warning signs and notices near timber harvesting operations and follow any signed diversions.

RUDLAND RIGG

The Rigg is situated with Farndale West on the east side and Bransdale on the west. To the south is the village of Gillamoor. Greenhow Moor and the Cleveland Way is to the North.

The trail along Rudland Rigg looking north.

Rudland Rigg is a ridge of wild countryside and beautiful scenic views. Bransdale to the west is only 5 miles long and one of the shortest dales in the area. To the east is Farndale, the valley famous for its vast spread of daffodils during spring.

Route (1) Follow the Barnsdale Road towards Cockayne. Opposite Cow Sike Farmyard (before the signposted Bridleway) turn right on to a well defined unsigned track. At the top of the hill turn right on to Westside Road a broad track along Rudland Rigg. The trig point is on your right where the views are magnificent both to the east towards Blakey Ridge and Helsmsley Moor to the west.

Route (2) From Cockayne cross the cattle grid, do not turn left at Breck House but keep straight on. At the second bridleway sign turn right, there is a plaque erected by the Nawton Tower Estate at the beginning of this bridleway. Travel in a northerly direction and turn left at the junction of trails going over Slape Wath Moor. At Medd Crag there is a definite crossing of tracks, turn right up the hill towards Round Hill and Bloworth Crossing, where you turn right onto the Rigg. After the remains of Cockam Cross follow the Rigg for approximately ¹⁄₂ mile and take the track down on your right to Cow Sike Farm.

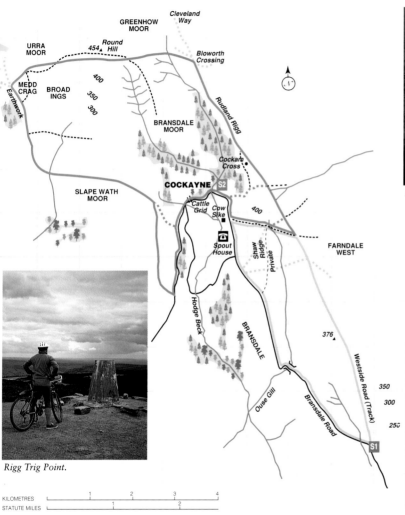

Map labels:
GREENHOW MOOR
Cleveland Way
Round Hill 454
URRA MOOR
Bloworth Crossing
MEDD CRAG
BROAD INGS
Earthwork
400
350
300
Rudland Rigg
BRANSDALE MOOR
Cockayne Cross
COCKAYNE S2
SLAPE WATH MOOR
Cattle Grid
Cow Sike
400
Spout House
Shaw Ridge
Private
FARNDALE WEST
Hodge Beck
BRANSDALE
Ouse Gill
376
Bransdale Road
Westside Road (Track)
350
300
250
S1

KILOMETRES 1 2 3 4
STATUTE MILES 1 2

Rigg Trig Point.

Autumn day on Ouse Gill.

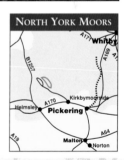

NORTH YORK MOORS
Whitby
A171
A169
B1257
Kirkbymoorside
Helmsley
A170
Pickering
A19
Malton
Norton
A64

START & FINISH (1)	[S] Junction of Westside Road (track) and Bransdale Road
(2)	Cockayne Village
MAP :	O.S. Outdoor Leisure 26, North York Moors (West)
LENGTH (approx) :	(1) 11 km (7 m) Circular
	(2) 22 km (14 m) Circular
SURFACE :	Rough moorland/gravel/tarmac
RIDE RATING :	(1) & (2) Moderate Adventurous

NOTES : Care must be taken of the ever changing weather conditions on the high moorlands. Between August and October you may encounter grouse shooting parties on Rudland Rigg.

BOLTBY FOREST

THE FOREST IS SITUATED NORTH EAST OF THIRSK ON THE EDGE OF HAMBLETON HILLS WITH HAMBLETON OLD DROVE ROAD RUNNING TO THE EAST OF THE TRAILS. THE ROAD FROM FELIXKIRK TO HAWNBY IS TO THE SOUTH.

Boltby Forest is mainly a conifer woodland, first planted in 1929 and covers an area of 500 hectares. Although the routes are quite testing it is well worth climbing to one of the higher points in the forest as the views over the northern Vale of York are wonderful.

Forest Enterprise

Forest Enterprise part of the Forestry Commission

Forest Enterprise woods are managed with multi-purpose objectives, including conservation, recreation and the production of a sustainable supply of timber. Please obey any warning signs and notices near timber harvesting operations and follow any signed diversions.

START & FINISH S	High Paradise Farm (no parking) see notes	
MAP :	O.S. Outdoor Leisure 27 North York Moors (West)	
LENGTH (approx) :	Green Trail	6 ½ km (4 m) Circular
	Red Trail	11 km (7 m) Circular
	Blue Trail	19 ½ km (12 m) Circular
SURFACE :	Forest tracks/gravel	
RIDE RATING :	Route 1 (Green)	Moderate
	Route 2 (Red)	Hard
	Route 3 (Blue)	Hard

NOTES : *The forest will be closed on pheasant shoot days. These days are displayed at High Paradise Farm* N.B. All parking is at top of Sneck Yate Bank.

KILOMETRES

STATUTE MILES

| 1 | 2 | 3 | 4 |

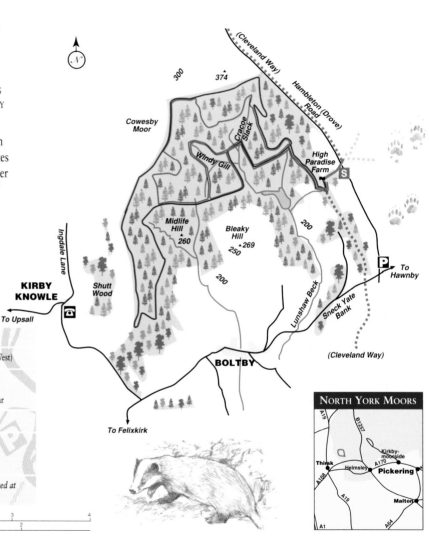

LANGDALE FOREST

THIS FOREST IS BORDERED BY THE A169 PICKERING TO SLEIGHTS
ROAD TO THE WEST AND THE RIVER DERWENT ON THE EASTERN
BOUNDARY OF THE FOREST. FYLINGDALE MOORS ARE TO THE
NORTH AND DALBY FOREST TO THE SOUTH.

Other than the tracks that are waymarked, with a little
navigation, there are numerous other tracks in the 4500
hectares of forest for the adventurous rider. The highest
point in the north being High Woof Howe at 280 m.
   The ride up to the Cross on Lilla Howe will be
rewarded with exceptional views of the surrounding
moorlands, at the point where the track cuts across the
route of the long distance 'Lyke Wake Walk'. The Cross
is said to mark the burial place of a Saxon nobleman
who died saving the life of the King by throwing himself
on the sword of the assassin.

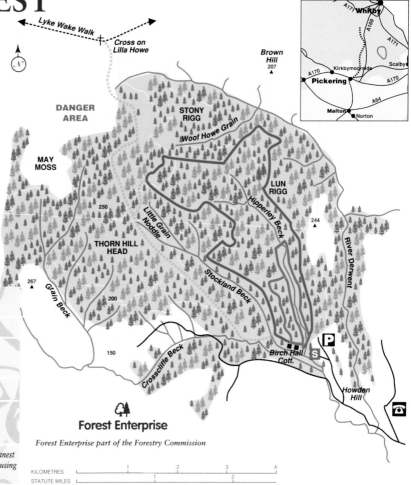

START & FINISH (all routes)	S	Hipperley Beck Entrance. Car park at Birch Hall
MAP :		O.S. Outdoor Leisure 27 North York Moors (East)
LENGTH (approx) :		Purple Trail 6 ½ km (4 m) Circular
		To Lilla Howe 9km (5 ½ m) Linear
		Green trail 13 km (8 m) Circular
SURFACE :		Forest tracks/gravel/grass
RIDE RATING :		Route 1 (Purple) Moderate
		Route 2 (Green) Hard
		To Lilla Howe (Brown) Hard

NOTES : All streams in Langdale Forest feed into the R. Derwent, one of Englands cleanest
and most environmentally sensitive rivers. Cyclists should avoid riding in streams and causing
unnecessary muddying. Park at start of trails at Birch Hall.

Forest Enterprise

Forest Enterprise part of the Forestry Commission

Cliffs at Ravenscar (inset looking across Robin Hood's Bay from Ravenscar).

'WHITBY WILLIE'
SCARBOROUGH TO WHITBY

THIS TRAIL IS SITUATED BETWEEN SCARBOROUGH AND WHITBY OVERLOOKING THE
NORTH SEA TO THE EAST AND THE NORTH YORKSHIRE MOORS TO THE WEST.

Class W Tank Engine "Whitby Willie".

START :	S	Scalby, Nr. Scarborough
FINISH :		Hawsker, Nr. Whitby
MAP :		O.S. Outdoor Leisure 27 North Yorks Moors (East)
LENGTH (approx) :		28 km (17½ m) Linear (Scalby-Hawsker) 32 km (20 m) Linear (Scarborough-Whitby)
SURFACE :		Gravel/tarmac
RIDE RATING :		Moderate

The views along this trail are unsurpassable, the track is the bed of the old railway line and is high above the sea coast, in places overlooking the North Sea. The track descending towards Robin Hood's Bay used to be so steep and twisty a special type of engine, the Class W tank engine, was built for the route, it was nicknamed the 'Whitby Willie'.

The Scarborough to Whitby Railway Company completed in 1885 and over the 80 years that it was open, large numbers of people travelled between the two towns, mainly on holiday excursions. Commencing from Scalby, Ravenscar is the summit of the hill which is 631ft above sea level. The railway engines could only average a speed of 20 miles an hour and therefore, earned the nickname of the 'Steep & Winding Railway'. Due to lack of funds to keep the railway going the Scarborough & Whitby Railway was axed by Beeching in March 1965.

The route starts off Station Road, on Field Close Road, Scalby. Follow the signs for the "Railway Walk" down Lancaster Way to the end and turn right between two houses onto the old railway track to Burniston village.

33

WHITBY WILLIE

At Ravenscar the cliffs rise to 585ft and have been altered considerably by the alum quarries, worked in 1640. Back in the 3rd and 4th centuries there was a Roman fort there, where later the Danes invaded and hoisted their flag bearing a raven's image. Ravenscar is also the finishing point of the 40 mile Lyke Wake walk which starts in Osmotherley on the western edge of the North York Moors.

The trail is easy to follow, with the exception of the detour at Ravenscar. Robin Hood's Bay was known as Robbyn Huddes Bay in the Tudor times, but the locals prefer to call it Bay Town. Apart from the smuggling of tea, brandy and tobacco during the 18th century, the village thrived on fishing and could boast a registered fleet of 174 boats during the early 1800s.

After Robin Hood's Bay, Hawsker was the last railway station before crossing the 13 arch Viaduct, 120ft above the River Esk, to the terminal at Prospect Hill where passengers could further their journey via this junction to Middlesbrough.

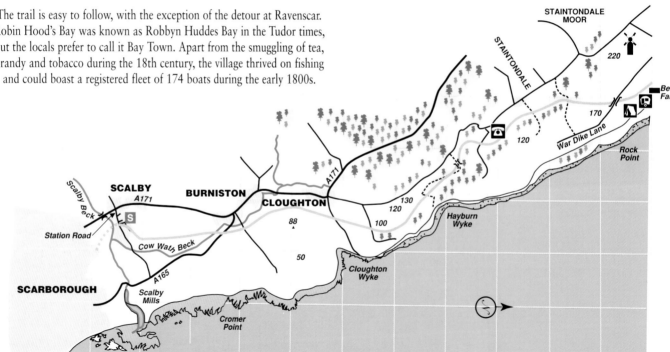

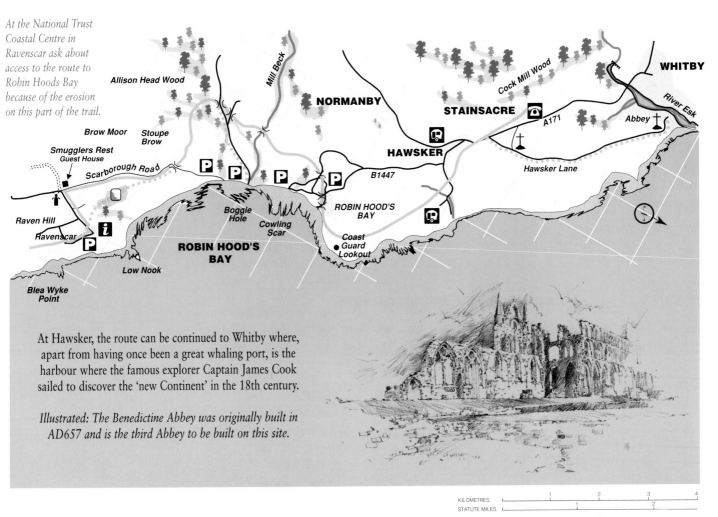

*At the National Trust
Coastal Centre in
Ravenscar ask about
access to the route to
Robin Hoods Bay
because of the erosion
on this part of the trail.*

WHITBY

Allison Head Wood

Mill Beck

Cock Mill Wood

River Esk

NORMANBY

STAINSACRE

A171

Abbey

Brow Moor

Stoupe
Brow

HAWSKER

Smugglers Rest
Guest House

Scarborough Road

Hawsker Lane

Raven Hill

Boggle
Hole

B1447

ROBIN HOOD'S
BAY

Ravenscar

Cowling
Scar

ROBIN HOOD'S
BAY

Coast
Guard
Lookout

Low Nook

Blea Wyke
Point

At Hawsker, the route can be continued to Whitby where,
apart from having once been a great whaling port, is the
harbour where the famous explorer Captain James Cook
sailed to discover the 'new Continent' in the 18th century.

*Illustrated: The Benedictine Abbey was originally built in
AD657 and is the third Abbey to be built on this site.*

KILOMETRES   1   2   3   4
STATUTE MILES   1   2

CASTLE HOWARD

THE ESTATE OF CASTLE HOWARD LIES 15 MILES NORTH-EAST OF YORK IN THE HOWARDIAN HILLS AND WEST OF THE TOWN OF MALTON IN THE DISTRICT OF RYEDALE. THE B1257 LIES TO THE NORTH AND THE A64(T) TO THE SOUTH.

START & FINISH S	Castle Howard car park	
MAP :	O.S. Landranger 100 Malton, Pickering	
LENGTH (approx) :	22 km (14 miles) Circular The trail directly around the Castle is 14 km (8 ¾m)	
SURFACE :	Tarmac/gravel/grass	
RIDE RATING :	Moderate	

The grounds of Castle Howard cover an area of 1,000 acres and within this area there is a spectacular 70 acre lake. Around the Estate there are beautifully decorated monuments, a mausoleum and pyramid, all examples of the flamboyant wealth and powerful ambition of Charles Howard, 3rd Earl of Carlisle.

On this site in the eleventh century there was Henderskelfe Castle which was burnt down in 1693. The present castle is built on the site of the old village of Henderskelfe and was designed by John Vanburgh, who also designed Blenheim Palace. The mansion took 50 years to build and was final completed in 1759. The Castle is owned to this day by the four sons of Lord Howard of Henderskelfe who died in 1884, and continues to be lived in by one of the sons with his family.

The grounds are a masterpiece of sculptured landscaping, with the pyramid and Hawksmoor's Mausoleum easily seen from the trail. The bridleway along the wooded crest, north of the Castle, has magnificent views across the Vale of Pickering and the North York Moors.

Castle Howard - setting for the TV series "Brideshead Revisited".

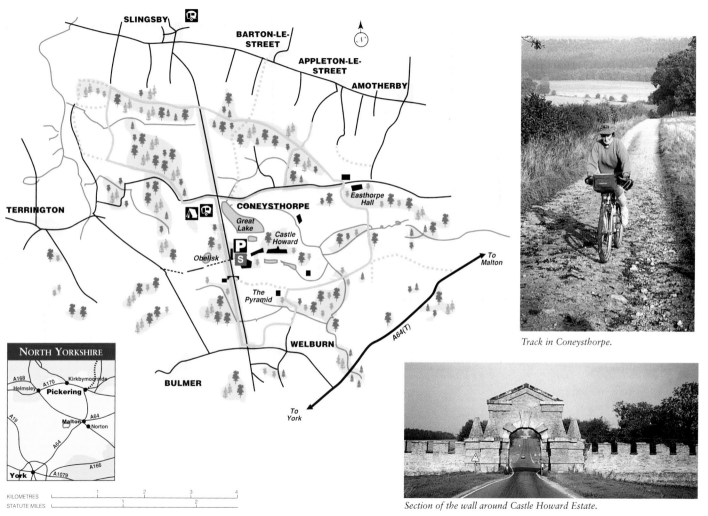

SLINGSBY

BARTON-LE-STREET

APPLETON-LE-STREET

AMOTHERBY

TERRINGTON

CONEYSTHORPE

Easthorpe Hall

Great Lake

Castle Howard

Obelisk

The Pyramid

WELBURN

To Malton

A64(T)

To York

BULMER

NORTH YORKSHIRE

A168
A170 Kirkbymoorside
Helmsley
Pickering
A19
A64
Malton Norton
A166
York
A1079

KILOMETRES   1   2   3   4
STATUTE MILES   1   2

Track in Coneysthorpe.

Section of the wall around Castle Howard Estate.

SINNINGTON TRIANGLE

SINNINGTON IS MIDWAY BETWEEN PICKERING AND KIRKBYMOORSIDE ON A MINOR ROAD OFF THE A170. THE TRAIL IS SITUATED SOUTH OF SPAUNTON MOOR AND TO THE EAST OF HUTTON-LE-HOLE.

The trail begins in Sinnington, a very attractive village with the River Seven flowing through and a tiny packhorse bridge in the middle of the broad green. Take the road over the bridge, turning right onto the bridleway and follow the track beside the river through the woods. Cross the field and turn left up the hill towards Appleton-le-Moors. Through the farm at Appleton-le-Moors and up Kirkgate Lane to Lastingham, with its fine church and 'ghostly' crypt. (For a shortened circuit turn left after Appleton-le-Moors onto Hamley Lane and follow the bridleway signs past Appleton Mill Farm to Sinnington)
To complete the full triangle, follow the road out of Lastingham to Cropton village, which lies on the edge of the vast Cropton Forest. Once over the bridge at Cropton Beck, turn right down a lane and follow the signposted bridleway through the woods, past the little Norman church, back to the village of Sinnington.

START & FINISH **S**	Sinnington
MAP :	O.S. Landranger 100 Malton, Pickering
LENGTH (approx) :	12 km (8m) Circular
SURFACE :	Tarmac/forest tracks
RIDE RATING :	Easy Adventurous

NOTES : *Park with care in the village of Sinnington*

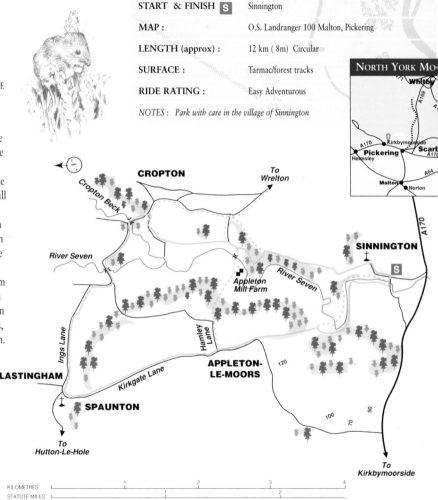

Trail in the woods above Sinnington.

HORNSEA RAIL TRAIL

THE TRAIL LIES WEST OF THE A165 THE HULL TO BRANDESBURTON ROAD AND EAST OF THE NORTH SEA COAST AT HORNSEA.

Our route commences on the site of Skirlaugh's former railway station. The original railway line opened in 1864 and closed 100 years later in October 1964. The line was known as 'Lakeland by the Sea', the freshwater lake being Hornsea Mere. The trail passes through peaceful farmlands of Holderness with sections designated as nature reserves for many of the wildlife that have taken up residence in the banks of the old railway.

START :	**S** Car Park and picnic area off the A165 south of Skirlaugh
FINISH :	Hornsea
MAP :	O.S. Landranger 107 Kingston upon Hull
LENGTH (approx) :	10km (6 1/2 m) Linear
SURFACE :	Gravel/tarmac
RIDE RATING :	Easy

NOTES : Due to some of the railway bridges missing over the roads, care must be taken at the road crossings along the trail.

KILOMETRES 1 2 3 4
STATUTE MILES 1 2

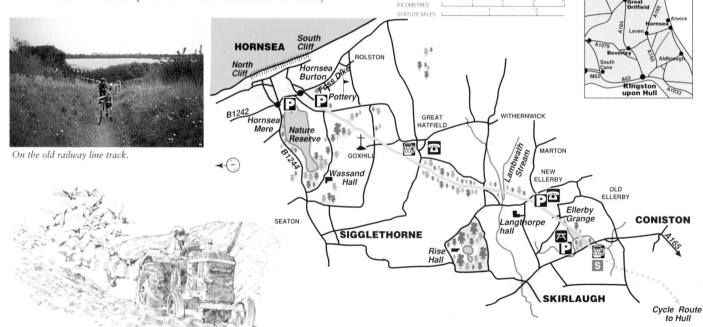

On the old railway line track.

40

HUDSON WAY
(BEVERLEY - MARKET WEIGHTON)

THIS ROUTE IS SITUATED IN EAST YORKSHIRE IN THE WOLDS BETWEEN THE
MARKET TOWNS OF BEVERLEY AND MARKET WEIGHTON. TO THE SOUTH IS
THE A1079 YORK TO HULL TRUNK ROAD.

START :	**S**	Molescroft, Nr. Beverley
FINISH :		Market Weighton (Springdale Road, turning off the A1079 opposite the School).
MAP :		O.S. Landranger 106 Market Weighton
LENGTH (approx) :		16 ½ km (11 m) Linear
SURFACE :		Gravel
RIDE RATING :		Easy

NOTES : Care to be taken at the road crossings where the old railway line bridges have
been demolished. The last mile of the Hudson Way into Market Weighton town centre is a
footpath.

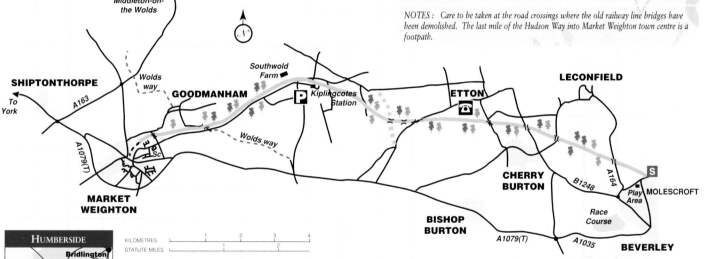

This trail was named after George Hudson who first
planned this York to Hull railway line in 1842.
The line was finally closed in 1965, having been a
successful N.E.Railway line for over a 100 years. The
banks and tracks of the old railway line have, in two
different sections of the route, been designated a nature reserve
and looked after by the Yorkshire Naturalist Trust.
The Wolds, with its gentle rolling hills, give this trail its
very relaxing and enjoyable character. Kiplingcotes Station
is the highest point on your trail, where you can stop for
refreshment knowing you are only 3 ½ miles from the
end of your route.

SPURN HEAD 'SAIL' RAILWAY

SPURN HEAD IS SITUATED AT THE MOUTH OF THE HUMBER AS IT MEETS THE
NORTH SEA. A SPIT OF LAND JUTTING SOUTH OFF THE NORTH BANK OF THE
RIVER WITH THE LIFEBOAT AND HUMBER PILOT STATION HOUSED ON THE TIP
OF THE PENINSULAR.

START & FINISH S	Kilnsea, Canal Scrape Hide Car Park
MAP :	O.S. Landranger 113 Grimsby
LENGTH (approx) :	7 km (3½m) Linear
SURFACE :	Sand/concrete
RIDE RATING :	Easy

Spurn Head is a peninsular of sand owing its
existence to the continual fight between the forces of
the sea and estuary currents. The wonderful peace
and quite of this wilderness is only broken by the
screeching of the sea birds and the noise of the wind as it blows the sand
across the road. Around the remains of the old railway workings, there is a
nature reserve managed by The Yorkshire Wildlife Trust.

This peninsular hides a wonderful history of at least a dozen lighthouses.
Lit through the ages by 'stone coal', then by oil, and finally, when electricity
reached this most south easterly tip of Yorkshire it was used for the
lighthouse as well as the inhabitants on Spurn Head.

In the early days between the two world wars, when the trains were not
running, the Lifeboatmen and War Department personnel, used two small
trolleys as the cheapest means of getting to and from Kilnsea for a pint or
two at the Blue Bell Inn. These trolleys had a lug sail mounted on a mast
from the back of the deck of the 'bogie' to propel them.
The passengers sat on the decking and with no brakes, other than dropping a
heavy piece of wood in front of the wheels, it was definitely a very
precarious method of travel, but infinitely preferable to walking
the 3½ miles.

The military occupied this area for coastal defence during both World Wars and a magnificent single track railway was built primarily to transport materials needed for building both the sea wall at Kilnsea, around 1915 and the WD installations along the peninsular. The railway disappeared during the terrible winter storms of 1951.

Spurn Head peninsular.

Spurn Head light house.

KILOMETRES

STATUTE MILES

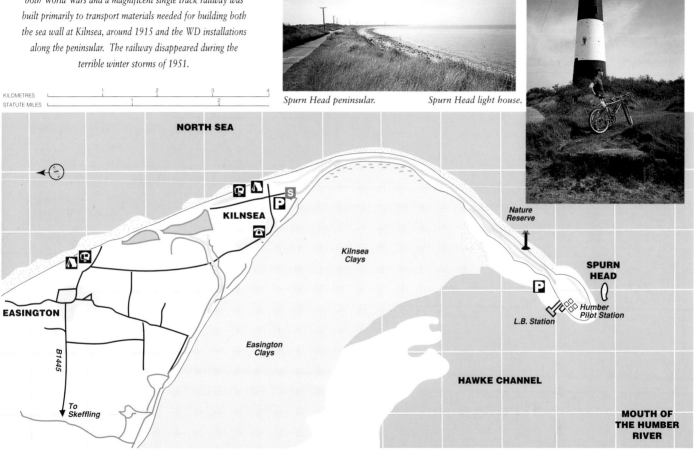

NORTH SEA

KILNSEA

EASINGTON

B1445

To
Skeffling

Kilnsea
Clays

Easington
Clays

Nature
Reserve

SPURN
HEAD

L.B. Station

Humber
Pilot Station

HAWKE CHANNEL

MOUTH OF
THE HUMBER
RIVER

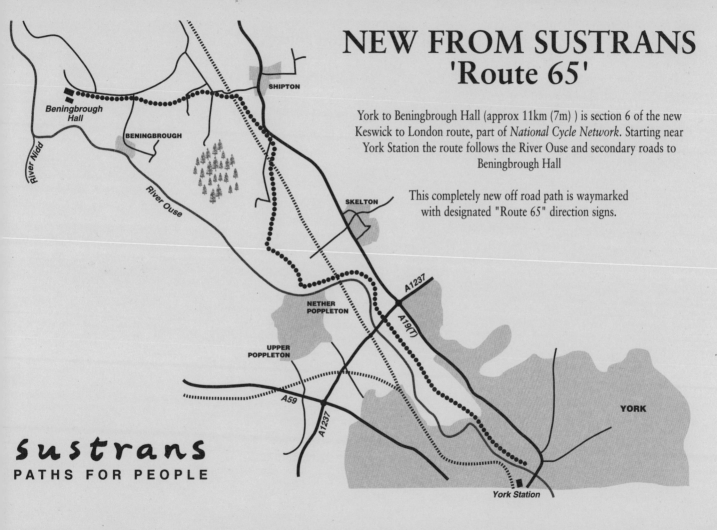

NEW FROM SUSTRANS
'Route 65'

York to Beningbrough Hall (approx 11km (7m)) is section 6 of the new Keswick to London route, part of *National Cycle Network*. Starting near York Station the route follows the River Ouse and secondary roads to Beningbrough Hall

This completely new off road path is waymarked with designated "Route 65" direction signs.

SHIPTON

Beningbrough Hall

BENINGBROUGH

SKELTON

River Nidd

River Ouse

A1237

A19(T)

NETHER POPPLETON

UPPER POPPLETON

A59

A1237

YORK

sustrans
PATHS FOR PEOPLE

York Station

45

CYCLE HIRE CENTRES

The following is a list of cycle hire centres. Intending hirers should telephone for opening times and types of bikes available.

YORKSHIRE DALES

Ian O. Rawlins
Woodburn Garage
(Next to Crown Inn)
ASKRIGG
Tel: (01969) 650455

Mountain Bike Hire
(Hardware Shop)
5 Chapel Street
GRASSINGTON
Tel: (01756) 752592

Phil Webster
Bike of Beyond
Grinton Lodge
(Youth Hostel)
GRINTON
Nr. Richmond
Tel: (01748) 884206

Three Peaks Mountain Bikes
HORTON-IN-RIBBLESDALE
Tel: (01729) 860200

Kettlewell Garage
KETTLEWELL
Tel: (01756) 760225

NORTH YORKSHIRE

Dave Ferguson Cycles
48 High Street
GARGRAVE
Tel: (01756) 795367

Dalesman Cafe
54 High Street
GARGRAVE
Tel: (01756) 795367

Bike It!
Gales House Farm
GILLAMOOR
Tel: (01751) 431258

The Outdoor Shop
Borogate
HELMSLEY
Tel: (01439) 770886

Mad Mole Mountain Bikes
25 Yorkersgate
MALTON
Tel: (01653) 690073

Ryed-a-bike
Mountain Bike Hire
MALTON
Tel: (01653) 692835

Golden Square Caravan Park
OSWALDKIRK
Nr. Helmsley
Tel: (01439) 788269

Mike Todd
Adventure Leisure
Mill Activity Centre, Glasshouses
NR. PATELEY BRIDGE
Tel: (01423) 711209

Arthur Caygill Cycles (limited hire)
Gallowfields Trading Estate
Borough Road
RICHMOND
Tel: (01748) 825469

Bay Bike Hire
Glen Ray
Station Road
ROBIN HOOD'S BAY
Tel: (01947) 880488
  or (01947) 820326

Dave Ferguson Cycles
1 Brook Street
SKIPTON
Tel: (01756) 795367

Wardill Brothers
The Square
THORNTON DALE
Nr. Pickering
Tel: (01751) 474335

North Road Cycles
WHITBY
Tel: (01947) 820326

WEST YORKSHIRE

Watson Cairns & Co. Ltd.
157-158 Lower Briggate
LEEDS
Tel: (01532) 458081

Two Wheels Good
35 Call Lane
LEEDS
Tel: (01532) 456867

FOR FURTHER CYCLE HIRE CENTRES PLEASE
CONTACT THE FOLLOWING TOURIST
INFORMATION CENTRES

Pickering	01751 73791
Beverley	01482 867430
Hull	01482 223559
York	01904 726331
Skipton	01756 792809
Hebden Bridge	01422 843831

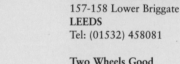

ACCOMMODATION GUIDE

This accommodation guide has been vetted for the suitability of cyclists and their bicycles, and has been selected from the combined guides from various Tourist Information Centres. For further information on accommodation contact the Information Centres, Telephone numbers on page 46.

NORTH YORKSHIRE/DALES

Holme House Farm
Barden, Skipton, BD23 6AT
Telephone: (01756) 711636

Court Croft
Hebden, Skipton,
Church Lane, BD23 5DX Telephone: (01756) 753406

The George Inn
Hubberholme, Skipton, BD23 5JE
Telephone: (01756) 760223

Anglers' Cottage
Kilnsey, Skipton, BD23 5PS
Telephone: (01756) 752301

Langerton Farm
Thorpe Lane, Linton, Skipton, BD23 5HN
Telephone: (01756) 730260

Bruce House
Top Wath Road, Pateley Bridge, Harrogate HG3 5PG
Telephone: (01423) 711813

Greengarth
Greenwood Road, Pateley Bridge, HG3 5LR
Telephone: (01423) 711688

Nappa Hall
Askrigg, Leyburn, DL8 3JZ
Telephone: (01969) 650260

Mrs Gillian Bowe
Cubble Head, Burtersett, Hawes, DL8 3PL
Telephone: (01969) 667714

High Bank House
31 East Lane, Embsay, Skipton, BD23 6QX
Telephone: (01756) 799197

Greenbank
Stirton-with-Thorlby, Skipton, BD23 3LH
Telephone: (01756) 793716

Bond Croft Farm
Embsay, Skipton, BD23 6SF
Telephone: (01756) 793371

Rockwood House
14 Main Street, Embsay, Skipton, BD23 6RE
Telephone: (01756) 799755

The Mason's Arms
Eastby, Nr. Skipton, BD23 6SN
Telephone: (01756) 792754

Sawley House
East Marton, Skipton, BD23 3LP
Telephone: (01282) 843207

Jeff & Christine Bottomley
West Marton, Nr. Skipton BD23 3UE
Telephone: (01282) 842402

Lindon Guest House
Airton, Nr. Skipton, BD23 4BE
Telephone: (01729) 830418

Coachmans Cottage
Hanlith, Malham, Nr. Skipton, BD23 4BP
Telephone: (01729) 830538

Wenningber Farm
Hellifield, Skipton, BD23 4JR
Telephone: (01729) 850856

The Oast Guest House
5 Pen-y-ghent View, Church Street, Settle, BD24 9JJ

Littledale Croft
Malham Road, Hellifield, Skipton, BD23 4JN
Telephone: (01729) 850894

South House
Selside, Horton-in-Ribblesdale, Settle, BD24 OHU
Telephone: (01729) 860271

Middle Studfold Farm
Horton-in-Ribblesdale, Settle BD24 OER
Telephone: (01729) 860236

The Corncrake
Cracoe, Nr. Skipton, BD23 6LA
Telephone: (01756) 730205

Fold Farm
Kettlewell, Skipton, BD23 5RH
Telephone: (01756) 760886

Bushey Lodge Farm
Starbotton, Skipton, BD23 5HY
Telephone: (01756) 760424

Moor End Farm
Langbar, Nr Bolton Abbey LS29 OEW
Telephone: (01943) 603109

Hesketh House Farm
Bolton Abbey, Skipton, BD23 6HA
Telephone: (01756) 710332

Langerton Farm
Linton, Skipton, BD23 5HN
Telephone: (01756) 730260

Whittakers Barn Farm
Cracoe, Skipton, BD23 6LB
Telephone: (01756) 730287

Court Croft
Church Lane, Hebden, Skipton, BD23 5DX
Telephone: (01756) 753406

Holly Tree Farm
Thorpe, Skipton, BD23 6BJ
Telephone: (01756) 720604

Grange Cottage
Linton, Skipton, BD23 5HH
Telephone: (01756) 752527

Grisedale Farm
Threshfield, Skipton, BD23 5NT
Telephone: (01756) 752516

Farfield
Wharfeside Avenue, Threshfield, Skipton, BD23 5BS
Telephone: (01756) 752435

Foresters Arms
Main Street, Grassington, Skipton,
Telephone: (01756) 752349

Springroyd House
8A Station Road, Grassington, Skipton, BD23 5NQ
Telephone: (01756) 752473

ACCOMMODATION GUIDE

Lodge Guest House
8 Wood Lane, Grassington, Skipton BD23 5LU
Telephone: (01756) 752518

Kirkfield
Hebden Road, Grassington, Skipton
Telephone: (01756) 752385

The George Inn
Hubberholme
Telephone: (01756) 760223

Kirkgill Manor
Hubberholme, Skipton, BD23 5JE
Telephone: (01756) 760800

Ampleforth Lodge
Country House, Ampleforth, York, YO6 4DA
Telephone: (01439) 788789

Pinewood Farm
Melbourne Road, Thornton,
Nr. Melbourne, York, YO4 4RJ
Telephone: (01759) 318351

'Blacksmith's Arms'
Seaton Ross, York, YO4 4LU
Telephone: (01759) 318781

NORTH YORKSHIRE MOORS

The Old Manse
Middleton Road Pickering YO18 8ALM
Telephone: (01751) 476484

Heathcote House
100 Eastgate Pickering YO18 7DW
Telephone: (01751) 476991

Moordale House
Rosedale East Pickering YO18 8RN
Telephone: (01751) 417219

Appleton Farmhouse
Appleton-le-Moors , YO6 6TE
Telephone: (01751) 417275

Lower Barn
Wandales Lane Bulmer, YO6 7ES
Telephone: (01653) 618575

Hollins Lodge
Farndale Kirkbymoorside, YO6 6LH
Telephone: (01751) 433436

South View
Gillamoor Kirkbymoorside YO6 6HX
Telephone: (01751) 431934

Cartoft Lodge
Keldholme Kirkbymoorside YO6 6NU
Telephone: (01751) 431566

Grindale House
123 Eastgate Pickering YO18 7DW
Telephone: (01751) 476636

Rosebank
61 Ruffa Lane Pickering YO18 7HN
Telephone: (01751) 472531

Green Lea
Sinnington, YO6 6SH
Telephone: (01751) 432008

Low Dalby House
Low Dalby, Thornton-le-Dale, Nr. Pickering YO18 7LT
Telephone: (01751) 460279

Rains Farm
Allerston Pickering YO18 7PQ
Telephone: (01723) 859333

Appleton Mill Farm
Appleton-le-Moors, YO6 6TG
Telephone: (01751) 417212

Rectory Farm
Levisham Pickering YO18 7NL
Telephone: (01751) 460304

Barn Close Farm
Rievaulx Helmsley YO6 5LH
Telephone: (01439) 798321

Ravine Cottage Guest House
16 Scarborough Road, Filey, YO14 9EF
Telephone: (01723) 514656

Orchard Farm Holiday Village
Hunmanby, Filey, YO14 0PU Telephone: (01723) 891582

Casablanca Hotel
20 Ryndleside, Scarborough YO12 6AD
Telephone: (01723) 362288

Oakleaf Holiday Flats
26 Ramshill Road, Scarborough, YO11 2QF
Telephone: (01944) 758888

Wayside Farm
Whitby Road, Cloughton, Scarborough,
YO13 0DX Telephone: (01723) 870519

The Grainary
Keasbeck Hill Farm, Harwood Dale,
YO13 0DT Telephone: (01723) 870026

East Farm Country Cottages
Scalby Nabs, Scalby, Scarborough, YO13 0SL
Telephone: (01723) 871011

WEST YORKSHIRE

Prospect House
North Road, Sutton-in-Craven, BD20 7PQ
Telephone: (01535) 632075.

Lumb Beck Farmhouse
Moorside, Addingham
Telephone: (01943) 830400

Windsover Farm
Middleton, Ilkley, LS29 0EF
Telephone: (01943) 600089

HUMBERSIDE

The New Inn
Leven, Beverley HU17 5NZ
Telephone: (01964) 542223

Oak House Guest House
43 North Bar Without, Beverley HU17 7AGC.
Telephone: (01482) 881481.

Cherry Tree Hotel
17 Flamborough Road, Bridlington YO15 2HU.
Telephone: (01262) 676852.

Park Avenue Hotel
Park Avenue, Bridlington YO15 2JJ.
Telephone: (01262) 674133.

Pinderhill Farm
Beeford, Driffield
Telephone: (01262) 488645

ACCOMMODATION GUIDE

Park Farm House
Main Road, Burton Agnes, Nr. Driffield, YO25 ONA
Telephone: (01262) 490394.

Redstone Walk Farm
South Cave, Brough, HU15 2AH
Telephone: (01430) 422230.

Sefton Guest House
6 Bannister Street, Withernsea HU19 2DU
Telephone: (01964) 613523.

The Wolds Inn
Huggate, York, YO4 2YH
Telephone: (01377) 288217

The Old Mill Hotel and Restaurant
Mill Lane, Langtoft, Near Driffield, YO25 OBQ
Telephone: (01377) 267284.

The Triton Inn
Sledmere, Nr. Driffield, YO25 OXQ
Telephone: (01377) 236644.

Sedgwick Country Guesthouse
Park Street, Hovingham, YO6 4JZ
Telephone: (01653) 628740

Hobground
Great Barugh Malton YO17 OXD
Telephone: (01751) 431988

Ashburnham Guest House
1 Victoria Avenue, Hornsea, HU18 1NH
Telephone: (0964) 535118

Corner Cottage Hotel
Blacksmiths Corner Easington HU12 OTN
Telephone: (0964) 650268

Honeysuckle Farm
Bewholme Lane Hornsea HU18 1BY
Telephone: (0964) 533873

Rectory Farm Guest House/Restaurant
Blacksmiths Corner, Easington HU12 OTN
Telephone: (0964) 650280

St Hildas Guest House
40 The Promenade Withernsea HU19 2DW
Telephone: (0964) 612483

George and Dragon
High Street, Aldbrough HU11 4RP
Telephone: (0964) 527230

Granby Inn
North Church Side Easington HU12 OTW
Telephone: (0964) 650294

Kings Head
2 Souttergate, Hedon, HU12 8JS
Telephone: (0482) 899314

Marine Hotel
The Promenade Withernsea HU19 2DP
Telephone: (0964) 612434

Eastgate Guest House
7 Eastgate, Beverley, HU17 ODR
Telephone: (01482) 868464

Rose Villa Guest House
6 Hull Bridge Road Beverley
Telephone: (01482) 861461/862351

Buck Inn
25 Beckside, Beverley
Telephone: (01482) 868262

Beverley Friary Youth Hostel
The Friary, Friars Lane, Beverley HU17 ODF
Telephone: (01482) 881751

Arras Farmhouse
Arras, Market Weighton, York, YO4 3RN
Telephone: (01430) 872404

Canal Head
Pocklington
Telephone: (01759) 305238

Bainton Burrows Farm
Bainton, Driffield, YO25 9BJ
Telephone: (01377) 217202

Bishop Burton College of Agriculture
Bishop Burton, Beverley, HU17 9OG
Telephone: (01964) 550481

Clematis House
Eastgate, Lund, Driffield, YO25 9TQ
Telephone: (01377) 217204

ACCOMMODATION GUIDE

Crow Tree Farm
Arram, Nr. Leconfield, HU17 7NR
Telephone: (01964) 550167

Robeanne House Farm
Driffield Lane, Shiptonthorpe, YO4 5LB
Telephone: (01430) 873312

'Cairnlite'
60, Wod Lane, Beverley, HU17 8BS
Telephone: (01482) 867494

Mrs P Collman
4 Ellerker Road, Beverley, HU17 8LE
Telephone: (01482) 868617

Mrs Crompton
6 St Mary's Close, St Mary's Walk, Beverley, HU17 7AY
Telephone: (01482) 868837

Mrs King
1, Woodlands Beverley, HU17 8BT
Telephone: (01482) 862752

Mrs Lambie
45 Grove Park Beverley HU17 9JU
Telephone: (01482) 867871

Mrs Lindsey
2 Thurstan Road, Beverley,
Telephone: (01482) 881447

Mrs McDonald-Parry
109 Old Walkergate Beverley HU17 9BP
Telephone: (01482) 867705

Mrs Pratt
42 Holderness Crescent Beverley, HU17 OBE
Telephone: (01482) 867551

Mrs Whitelaw
"Northumbria" 13 The Croft, Molescroft, Beverley, HU17 7HT
Telephone: (01482) 872254

White Rose Cottage
230 Hull Bridge Road, Beverley
Telephone: (01482) 860191

Mrs Rigby
3 Norwood, Beverley
Telephone: (01482) 885177

Mrs Richley
60 St Leonards Road Molescroft Beverley
Telephone: (01482) 871249

Hemingford House
Church Street Welton, Brough, HU15 1NH
Telephone: (01482) 668405/668097

Mrs Scott
86 The Meadows, Cherry Burton
Telephone: (01964) 550331

Kenwood House
7 Newgate Street, Cottingham, HU16 4DY
Telephone: (01482) 847558

Mrs J Kirkman
99 Epplewoth Road, Cottingham HU16 5YG
Telephone: (01482) 841712

Turks Trod House
67A Church Street, South Cave, Brough, HU15 2EP
Telephone: (01430) 423931

Mrs Dorning
7 Wandby Close Walkington HU17 8SA
Telephone: (01482) 861249

Mrs England
1 All Hallows Road, Walkington, Nr. Beverley
Telephone: 01482 881775

Mrs J Gray
11 Northgate, Walkington, Nr. Beverley HU17 8ST
Telephone: (01482) 869911/867281

Mrs McCloskey
16 Meadow Way Walkington, Beverley
Telephone: (01482) 860542

Ronora
31 All Hallows Road, Walkington, HU17 8SH
Telephone: (01482) 862553

DISCLAIMER NOTICE:
IMPORTANT: Inclusion in this list does not imply recommendation by "Wilde's Guides" although efforts have been made to ensure the accuracy of this accommodation list. This is not an exclusive listing of cyclist vetted accommodation and many more apply, it is advisable to contact the Information Centre in the area concerned for further information.

HELP CREATE A TRAFFIC-FREE NETWORK...
Roads for people

- The figures speak for themselves. Over 20 million cars are registered in Britain and road traffic is projected to at least DOUBLE by the year 2025.

- Twice as much traffic on our roads.... What an appalling prospect!

- And the more cars there are, the more unpleasant it gets to travel by bike or on foot.

- But now, an alternative to the miseries of traffic-choked roads is being created...

THE SUSTRANS TRAFFIC-FREE NETWORK

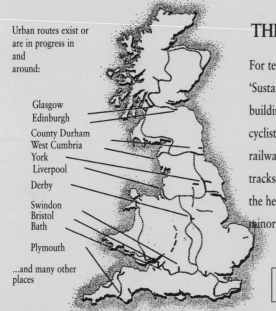

Urban routes exist or are in progress in and around:

Glasgow
Edinburgh
County Durham
West Cumbria
York
Liverpool
Derby
Swindon
Bristol
Bath
Plymouth
...and many other places

For ten years, Sustrans - it stands for 'Sustainable Transport' - has been building new traffic-free routes for cyclists and walkers, using disused railway lines, canal towpaths, forest tracks and riversides - often through the heart of towns and cities - linked to minor roads and open spaces.

The Sustrans paths are designed to make travel safer, healthier and more friendly for people and wildlife. They cut right through congestion and pollution. They are built where the need is greatest - in towns and cities with links to the countryside.

You can help bring about a complete national network! See overleaf for details.

KEY:	_____ Routes completed or in progress
	.... Main Sustrans proposals

sustrans
PATHS FOR PEOPLE

PLEASE JOIN SUSTRANS - AND HELP CREATE MORE TRAFFIC-FREE ROUTES

More public support and activity is needed to achieve a true national network. Without donations from the public, the routes simply would not happen.

Your contribution will be directly used to start new paths countrywide. Once we have done the initial work, we can often secure grants to cover the construction cost.

If you can give a donation, please be generous and in particular, consider making a regular commitment of a few pounds each month, to provide an income we can rely on.

Please use the Sustrans paths and tell others about them.

Sustrans routes are in progress between Dover and Inverness, between Bristol and London, across the Pennines and elsewhere.

PATRONS INCLUDE:

Chris Boardman • Dr Mayer Hillman • Dervia Murphy • Bill Oddie
Jeremy Paxman • Jonathan Porritt

sustrans
PATHS FOR PEOPLE

HEAD OFFICE 35 King Street, Bristol BS1 4DZ Tel: 0272 268893
SCOTLAND 53 Cochrane Street, Glasgow G1 1HL Tel: 041 552 8241
NORTH EAST Rockwood House, Barn Hill, Stanley,Co Durham DH9 8AN Tel: 0207 281259

Registered Charity No 326550 Company Limited by Guarantee No 1797726
VAT Registration No 416740656

Yes I'll join
Set of lovely Sustrans postcards free when you join

NAME ....
ADDRESS ....
....
POSTCODE .... PHONE ....

[ ] Please send information about Sustrans routes near me.

EITHER

YES I'll join with a donation of:
[£15] [£25] [£50] [£100] [£ ____ other] (please tick)

Please EITHER enclose cheque/PO payable to SUSTRANS OR complete you Access/Visa No. here and sign:

Card Expiry Date ....
Signature .... Date ....

_____ / _____ / _____ / _____

AND/OR

Even better for Sustrans, join with a regular monthly payment. We will send a beautiful wallmap of the paths - plus postcards - to thank you for your standing order of £3 a month or more.

YES I'll join with a monthly standing order of:
[£3] [£5] [£10] [£15] [£25]
[£_____other] (please tick)

NAME OF MY BANK ....
ADDRESS OF MY BANK ....
....
Current Acc No _ /_ /_ /_ /_ /_ /_ /_ /_ /
Bank Sort Code _ /_ /-_ /_ /-_ /_ /

MY NAME ....
Signature .... Date ....

DON'T FORGET TO COMPLETE YOUR OWN ADDRESS ABOVE!
REMEMBER You can cancel this standing order at any time by informing your bank.
BANK INSTRUCTIONS: Please pay the above sum on the 1st next and monthly thereafter to SUSTRANS, Acc No 1400978, Lloyds Bank, 55 Corn St, Bristol BS99 7LE.
Sort Code 30-00-01.

POST TO SUSTRANS, FREEPOST BS7739, Bristol, BS1 4BR.
No stamp is required although it will save us paying postage if you use one.
Thank you

WILDE'S
LEISURE GUIDES

CYCLE ROUTE GUIDE

TO YORKSHIRE DALES, HUMBERSIDE, NORTH AND WEST YORKSHIRE

PLUS
LIST OF CYCLE HIRE CENTRES
& ACCOMMODATION GUIDE

34 LEISURE TRAILS